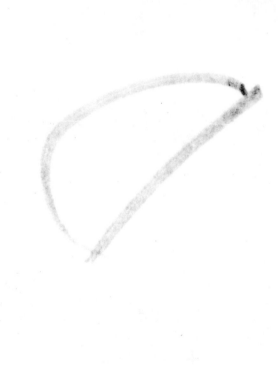

Water Habitats
Hábitats acuáticos

Wetlands/
Terrenos pantanosos

JoAnn Early Macken

Reading consultant/Consultora de lectura:
Susan Nations, M. Ed., author, literacy coach,
consultant/autora, tutora de alfabetización, consultora

Please visit our web site at: **www.earlyliteracy.cc**
**For a free color catalog describing Weekly Reader® Early Learning Library's list
of high-quality books, call 1-877-445-5824 (USA) or 1-800-387-3178 (Canada).
Weekly Reader® Early Learning Library's fax: (414) 336-0164.**

Library of Congress Cataloging-in-Publication Data available upon request from publisher.
Fax (414) 336-0157 for the attention of the Publishing Records Department.

ISBN 0-8368-6032-2 (lib. bdg.)
ISBN 0-8368-6039-X (softcover)

This edition first published in 2006 by
Weekly Reader® Early Learning Library
A Member of the WRC Media Family of Companies
330 West Olive Street, Suite 100
Milwaukee, WI 53212 USA

Copyright © 2006 by Weekly Reader® Early Learning Library

Art direction: Tammy West
Cover design and page layout: Kami Koenig
Picture research: Diane Laska-Swanke
Translators: Tatiana Acosta and Guillermo Gutiérrez

Picture credits: Cover, pp. 7, 15, 21 © Tom and Pat Leeson; pp. 5, 9, 19 © Alan &
Sandy Carey; p. 11 © Gustav Verderber/Visuals Unlimited; p. 13 © Bernard Castelein/
naturepl.com; p. 17 © Dr. Fred Hossler/Visuals Unlimited

Printed in the United States of America

1 2 3 4 5 6 7 8 9 09 08 07 06 05

Note to Educators and Parents

Reading is such an exciting adventure for young children! They are beginning to integrate their oral language skills with written language. To encourage children along the path to early literacy, books must be colorful, engaging, and interesting; they should invite the young reader to explore both the print and the pictures.

Water Habitats is a new series designed to help children read about the plants and animals that thrive in and around water. Each book describes a different watery environment and some of its resident wildlife.

Each book is specially designed to support the young reader in the reading process. The familiar topics are appealing to young children and invite them to read — and reread — again and again. The full-color photographs and enhanced text further support the student during the reading process.

In addition to serving as wonderful picture books in schools, libraries, homes, and other places where children learn to love reading, these books are specifically intended to be read within an instructional guided reading group. This small group setting allows beginning readers to work with a fluent adult model as they make meaning from the text. After children develop fluency with the text and content, the book can be read independently. Children and adults alike will find these books supportive, engaging, and fun!

— Susan Nations, M.Ed., author, literacy coach,
and consultant in literacy development

Nota para los maestros y los padres

¡Leer es una aventura tan emocionante para los niños pequeños! A esta edad están comenzando a integrar su manejo del lenguaje oral con el lenguaje escrito. Para animar a los niños en el camino de la lectura incipiente, los libros deben ser coloridos, estimulantes e interesantes; deben invitar a los jóvenes lectores a explorar la letra impresa y las ilustraciones.

Hábitats acuáticos es una nueva colección diseñada para que los niños lean textos sobre plantas y animales que viven en el agua o cerca de ella. Cada libro describe un medio acuático diferente y presenta a algunos de los animales y plantas que lo habitan.

Cada libro está especialmente diseñado para ayudar a los jóvenes lectores en el proceso de lectura. Los temas familiares llaman la atención de los niños y los invitan a leer —y releer— una y otra vez. Las fotografías a todo color y el tamaño de la letra ayudan aún más al estudiante en el proceso de lectura.

Además de servir como maravillosos libros ilustrados en escuelas, bibliotecas, hogares y otros lugares donde los niños aprenden a amar la lectura, estos libros han sido especialmente concebidos para ser leídos en un grupo de lectura guiada. Este contexto permite que los lectores incipientes trabajen con un adulto que domina la lectura mientras van determinando el significado del texto. Una vez que los niños dominan el texto y el contenido, el libro puede ser leído de manera independiente. ¡Estos libros les resultarán útiles, estimulantes y divertidos a niños y a adultos por igual!

— Susan Nations, M.Ed., autora/tutora de alfabetización/
consultora de desarrollo de la lectura

A **marsh** is a wetland. Plants called cattails grow in a marsh. Their flowers look like cats' tails. Their long, thin leaves wave in the wind.

Una **marisma** es un terreno pantanoso. En una marisma crecen unas plantas llamadas tules. Sus flores parecen la cola de un gato. Sus hojas largas y finas ondean al viento.

cattail/
tule

Muskrats build their homes from cattails, mud, and branches. They eat the cattail roots.

- - - - - - - - - - - - - - -

Las ratas almizcladas construyen sus hogares con tules, lodo y ramas. Se comen las raíces de los tules.

Birds eat cattails, too. Blackbirds build their nests among the **reeds**, or tall grasses.

También los pájaros comen tules. Los turpiales hacen sus nidos entre los **juncos** o hierbas altas.

cattail/
tule

9

A **bog** is a wetland. In a bog, moss grows on top of the water. Other plants grow on the moss.

- - - - - - - - - - - - - - -

Un **tremedal** es un terreno pantanoso. En un tremedal, el musgo crece sobre el agua. Otras plantas crecen sobre el musgo.

moss/
musgo

plant/planta

11

In a bog, some plants eat insects.
The plants catch insects in traps.

En un tremedal, algunas plantas
comen insectos. Las plantas
atrapan a los insectos con sus
trampas.

trap/trampa

A **swamp** is a wetland. Trees can grow in a swamp. Moss hangs down from the trees.

Un **pantano** es un terreno pantanoso. En un pantano pueden crecer árboles. De los árboles cuelga el musgo.

Mosquitoes hatch in a swamp.
Fish eat mosquitoes and their
young, or **larvae**.

- - - - - - - - - - - - - - -

En un pantano, los mosquitos
salen de los huevos. Los peces se
comen a los mosquitos y a las
crías, o **larvas**.

moss/musgo

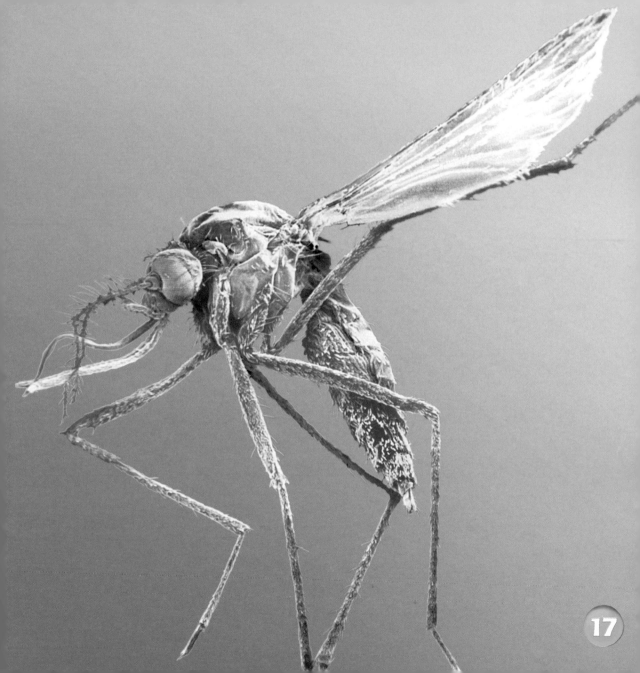

A heron wades on long, thin legs.
It looks for fish or frogs to eat.

--- --- --- --- --- --- --- --- --- --- --- --- ---

Una garza camina por el agua
sobre sus patas largas y finas.
Busca peces o ranas para comer.

Alligators live in swamps. They hunt under the water. Their jaws snap up prey. Watch out!

- - - - - - - - - - - - - - - -

Los caimanes viven en pantanos. Buscan comida bajo el agua. Atrapan a sus presas con sus mandíbulas. ¡Cuidado!

alligator/caimán

21

Glossary

hatch — to break out of an egg

mosquitoes — small buzzing insects that suck blood from animals

moss — small plants that grow in wet places

muskrats — rodents with shiny brown fur and long, thin tails

prey — an animal eaten by another animal

reeds — tall grasses that grow in wetlands

Glosario

juncos — hierbas altas que crecen en terrenos pantanosos

mosquitos — pequeños insectos voladores que chupan la sangre de otros animales

musgo — plantas muy pequeñas que crecen en lugares húmedos

presa — animal que es comido por otro animal

ratas almizcladas — roedores de pelo brillante color café y cola larga y delgada

For More Information/
Más información

Books in English

Living near the Wetland. Rookie Read-About Geography (series). Donna Loughran (Children's Press)

Wetlands. Biomes of North America (series). Lynn M. Stone (Rourke)

Libros en Español

El ciclo del agua/The Water Cycle. Helen Frost (Capstone)

La salamandra. Lola M. Schaefer (Heinemann)

Index

Índice

About the Author

JoAnn Early Macken is the author of two rhyming picture books, *Sing-Along Song* and *Cats on Judy*, and many other nonfiction books for beginning readers. Her poems have appeared in several children's magazines. A graduate of the M.F.A. in Writing for Children and Young Adults program at Vermont College, she lives in Wisconsin with her husband and their two sons. Visit her Web site at www.joannmacken.com.

Información sobre la autora

JoAnn Early Macken ha escrito dos libros de rimas con ilustraciones, *Sing-Along Song y Cats on Judy*, y muchos otros libros de no ficción para lectores incipientes. Sus poemas han sido publicados en varias revistas infantiles. JoAnn se graduó en el programa M.F.A. de Escritura para Niños y Jóvenes de Vermont College. Vive en Wisconsin con su esposo y sus dos hijos. Puedes visitar su página web: www.joannmacken.com

24